WEATHER AND CLIMATE

JOE GREEK

Britannica
Educational Publishing

IN ASSOCIATION WITH

ROSEN
EDUCATIONAL SERVICES

Published in 2018 by Britannica Educational Publishing (a trademark of Encyclopædia Britannica, Inc.) in association with The Rosen Publishing Group, Inc.
29 East 21st Street, New York, NY 10010

Distributed exclusively by Rosen Publishing.
To see additional Britannica Educational Publishing titles, go to rosenpublishing.com.

First Edition

Britannica Educational Publishing
J.E. Luebering: Executive Director, Core Editorial
Mary Rose McCudden: Editor, Britannica Student Encyclopedia

Rosen Publishing
Amelie von Zumbusch: Editor
Nelson Sá: Art Director
Nicole Russo-Duca: Designer & Book Layout
Cindy Reiman: Photography Manager
Nicole Baker: Photo Researcher

Library of Congress Cataloging-in-Publication Data

Names: Greek, Joe, author.
Title: Weather and climate / Joe Greek.
Description: New York : Britannica Educational Publishing, in Association with Rosen Educational Services, 2018. | Series: Let's find out! our dynamic earth | Audience: Grades 1–4. | Includes bibliographical references and index.
Identifiers: LCCN 2017019543| ISBN 9781680488425 (library bound : alk. paper) | ISBN 9781680488418 (pbk. : alk. paper) | ISBN 9781538300329 (6 pack : alk. paper)
Subjects: LCSH: Weather—Juvenile literature. | Climatology—Juvenile literature.
Classification: LCC QC981.3 .G736 2018 | DDC 551.5—dc23
LC record available at https://lccn.loc.gov/2017019543

Manufactured in the United States of America

CONTENTS

What Are Weather and Climate?

Weather is the daily state of the atmosphere, or air, in any given place. The weather is important to people. It affects their comfort, their food supply, and even their safety.

There are many elements that combine to create weather. They include temperature, wind, humidity, precipitation, and atmospheric pressure. These elements vary from region to region.

On rainy days, people often wear raincoats or use umbrellas to stay dry.

There are different climates around the world. Desert climates are usually hot and dry.

Climate is the weather found in a certain place over a long period of time. An area's climate determines what kinds of plants can grow and what kinds of animals can survive there. People use information about climates to decide which crops to plant, to prepare for natural disasters, and even to choose the best season for traveling to vacation spots.

COMPARE AND CONTRAST

How are weather and climate similar? In what ways are they different?

TEMPERATURE AND WIND

Temperature is one of the basic elements of weather. Temperature is how warm or cold it is outside. Temperatures often change with the time of day or year.

Wind is the movement of air near Earth's surface. Wind can be a light breeze or a wild gale. The most powerful wind happens during storms like tornadoes, cyclones, typhoons, and hurricanes.

Changes in the temperature of air, land, and water cause wind.

In many areas, cold temperatures occur only during the winter. In polar areas, it can be cold all year long.

Bangladesh has a tropical monsoon climate. This means heavy summer rains, which can lead to dangerous flooding.

THINK ABOUT IT

Think of the windiest day you experienced. What was the weather like that day?

When air flows over a warm surface, it heats up and rises. This leaves room for cooler air to flow in. The flowing air is wind.

Winds greatly affect the weather. They bring cool air into warm areas. They also can bring rain, snow, or even dust and sand. For example, in southern Asia, winds known as monsoons bring rain during the summer. This happens because cool, moist air from the ocean moves in over the warm land.

HUMIDITY AND CLOUDS

On a sunny day a wispy cloud can be a beautiful sight, but at other times a cloud can be a sign of storms to come. A cloud is made up of millions of tiny water droplets or ice crystals floating together in the air.

The air always contains water vapor—water in the form of gas—which is invisible. The amount of moisture in the air is known as humidity. The amount of water vapor that air can hold depends on the air's temperature. The cooler the air, the less water it can hold.

Even on a dry and sunny day, the clouds in the sky are filled with small droplets of rain or ice.

COMPARE AND CONTRAST

Colors of clouds can help tell if a storm will occur. How would you describe the difference between a fair weather cloud and a storm cloud?

When air cools, some of the water vapor condenses, or forms visible water droplets. The droplets form around tiny particles in the air, such as dust or sea salt. Near the ground, the condensed water vapor becomes fog. Up in the sky, it forms clouds.

Many factors can cause clouds to release the moisture they contain.

PRECIPITATION AND STORMS

Precipitation is water that falls from the sky. It is a part of Earth's endless water cycle. Precipitation comes in many forms, including rain, hail, sleet, and snow. The form precipitation takes depends

VOCABULARY

The **water cycle** describes the way water continues to change form as it moves above, within, and around Earth.

Earth's water is constantly being recycled in a process known as the water cycle.

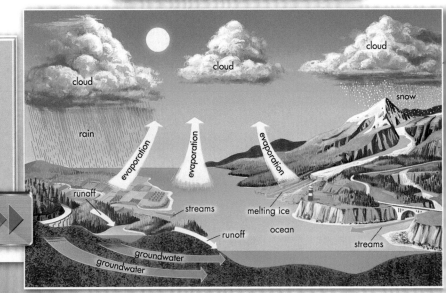

10

on other weather conditions, such as temperature.

Rain is liquid water that falls from the sky in drops. It forms in clouds that are made up of many water droplets. When the drops become too heavy to stay in the cloud, they fall to Earth as rain. Snow is tiny ice crystals that form inside a cloud when it is cold enough. When the ice crystals become too heavy to stay in the cloud, they fall to Earth as snow.

Precipitation fills lakes, ponds, rivers, and streams. It provides the fresh water needed by humans, animals, and plants. When too much precipitation falls, however, it can cause dangerous flooding. Too little precipitation can cause drought.

ATMOSPHERIC PRESSURE

Another element of weather is atmospheric pressure. Also known as barometric pressure, atmospheric pressure is the weight of air above a given area.

The atmospheric pressure is greatest at sea level. There, the gas particles are pressed together by the weight of the air above them. Air becomes lighter farther away from Earth's surface. As height increases, the air molecules become separated by more space, and the weight

Mountainous areas have lower atmospheric pressure than coastal areas.

Thunderstorms almost always include thick clouds, heavy rain, lightning, and strong winds.

decreases. As the weight of the air decreases, so does the air pressure. At sea level, air has a pressure of 14.7 pounds (6.7 kilograms) per square inch.

Changes in pressure help people to predict approaching storms. A storm is a disturbance in the atmosphere—for example, a thunderstorm or a hurricane.

THINK ABOUT IT

The human body gets the oxygen it needs from the air it breathes. Why do you think that people breathe faster and deeper on high mountains than they do at sea level?

Weather Forecasting

The weather on Earth is always changing. Meteorology is a field of science that studies the changes in weather on a day-to-day basis in a specific place. Scientists who study meteorology are called meteorologists.

Using various tools, meteorologists forecast whether it will rain or snow and whether it will be warm or cold. Meteorologists are often recognized as weathermen and women on television. However, most work in labs or outdoors.

Meteorologists use technology and tools to study weather patterns and predict possible storms.

COMPARE AND CONTRAST

What reasons do you have for needing to know the daily weather forecast? What other reasons might people have for needing a daily weather forecast?

Meteorologists use physics and chemistry to predict weather and how it will affect Earth. These forecasts are important to many people. For example, forecasts predicting when and where hurricanes will occur allow people who might be affected to prepare for the storm. Weather forecasts also help people who work in agriculture, in pollution control agencies, and in the aviation, maritime, and energy industries.

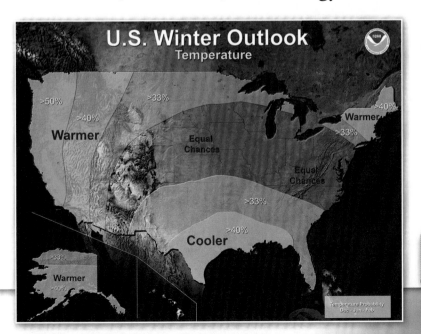

U.S. Winter Outlook
Temperature

>50%
>33%
>40%
>40%
Warmer
Warmer
>33%
Equal Chances
Equal Chances
>33%
>33%
>40%
Cooler
Warmer
>40%
Temperature Probability
Dec - Jan - Feb

The information gathered by meteorologists can be used to let people know whether it will be hot or cold.

WEATHER INSTRUMENTS

Before tools were developed to study weather, people predicted the weather based on their own observations. Today, meteorologists use many instruments to gather information about weather. The thermometer and the barometer are some of the oldest and most common weather instruments. The thermometer measures temperature, and the barometer measures atmospheric pressure. Another common instrument is the

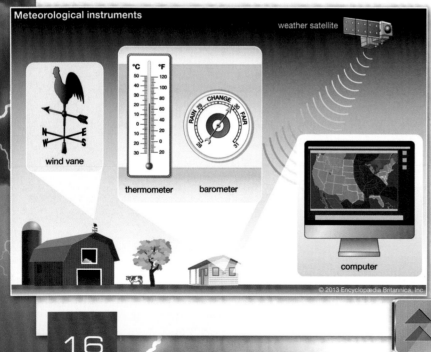

Meteorological instruments

wind vane

thermometer

barometer

weather satellite

computer

© 2013 Encyclopædia Britannica, Inc.

Meteorologists use a variety of instruments to collect information about weather.

wind vane, which shows the direction in which winds are blowing.

In the twentieth century, the computer became another valuable tool in meteorology. Computer programs use mathematics to create models of weather patterns. These models can forecast the weather 10 to 30 days ahead of time.

The first weather satellite was launched in 1960. Since then, meteorologists have used satellites to photograph weather systems, such as storms, around the world. The satellites also send weather data to meteorologists. Meteorologists continue to develop and use new technology, such as radar, to study the weather on Earth.

CLIMATE

Weather and climate are often confused. Weather is a short-term description of the air in an area. Climate is a long-term description of the weather in a region.

The study of climates is called climatology. Scientists have many tools to help in this study. They set up weather stations around Earth to measure rainfall, temperature, and wind speed. They send weather balloons with special instruments up into the atmosphere.

A scientist releases a weather balloon from a station located at the South Pole.

Think About It

Which statement describes weather and which describes climate: "It rained yesterday in Phoenix" or "Phoenix gets only 10 inches of rain per year"? What other statements can you think of to describe weather and climate?

Weather satellites in space also report information to scientists on the ground.

Climatologists study the elements of weather over long periods. They compile climate data each month and for the year as a whole. Some climatologists study how climates change over longer periods of time, such as hundreds or thousands of years. They use data from rocks and fossils, tree rings, and historical records.

Scientists can study the formation of tree rings to identify changes in climate over the years.

FACTORS THAT AFFECT CLIMATE

Many factors affect climate. These factors include the Sun, oceans, winds, land types, and clouds. Sunlight affects climate by hitting Earth unevenly. Places near the equator receive lots of strong sunlight throughout the year. This gives them a hot climate year-round. Places far from the equator are cooler.

Oceans also affect climate. Land near an ocean usually has a milder climate than an inland area. The ocean warms

The climate near Earth's poles is colder than other areas due to the way the Sun's rays hit the surface.

COMPARE AND CONTRAST

How are the effects of
winds and oceans on
climate similar? How are
they different?

the land in winter and cools
it in summer. Winds affect
climate by carrying warm or
cool air to areas. Winds also
bring different amounts
of moisture. The type of
land in an area affects the
climate, too. For example,
mountain ranges can block
cold air.

Clouds affect climate by blocking some of the heat
received from the Sun during the day. During the night,
clouds keep heat from escaping into space.

TYPES OF CLIMATES

No two places on Earth have exactly the same climate. Some of the general types of climates are tropical, subtropical, cyclonic, polar, and highland.

Tropical climates are warm all year and have no winter. They lie near the equator. Some tropical climates have a lot of rain. Others are dry. Subtropical climates are found north and south of the tropical climates. They have a greater range of temperatures than tropical climates. They also may be humid or dry. Cyclonic

The Amazon rainforest is located in a tropical climate, where it is warm all year.

climates are found mostly north of the equator. In these climates, people usually experience warmer summers and colder winters.

Polar climates are very cold. Snow and ice often cover the land. Highland, or mountain, climates have a great range of temperature between day and night. They tend to be humid and cooler than the lands nearby at a lower elevation.

Our planet has several types of climate, as shown on this map.

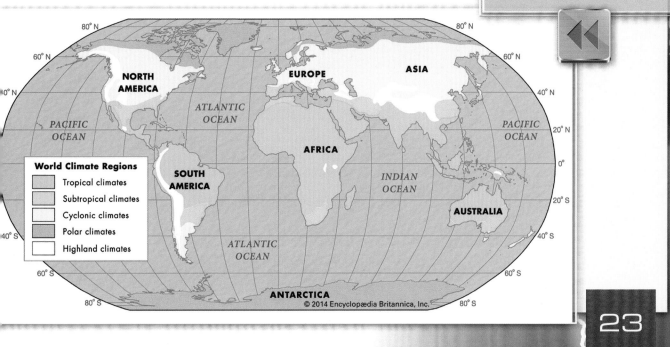

World Climate Regions
- Tropical climates
- Subtropical climates
- Cyclonic climates
- Polar climates
- Highland climates

© 2014 Encyclopædia Britannica, Inc.

CLIMATE CHANGE AND GLOBAL WARMING

Earth's climate changes over time. In the past, this was the result of natural forces and happened over long periods of time. Today, humans are affecting Earth's climate, causing it to change more quickly.

To understand climate change, it helps to understand the greenhouse effect. A greenhouse is a glass house where plants grow. Glass lets light in and keeps heat from escaping. Gases in Earth's atmosphere, called greenhouse gases, play a similar role for

The greenhouse gases released by fossil fuels damage Earth's atmosphere.

the planet as a whole. They trap heat near Earth. Without the greenhouse effect, Earth would be too cold for life to exist.

For much of Earth's history, greenhouse gases were not a problem. This changed as people came to depend on fossil fuels, such as oil and coal. The burning of fossil fuels to run cars and heat homes releases large amounts of greenhouse gases into the air. Scientists think that Earth is getting warmer because of the extra greenhouse gases in the air. This is known as global warming.

Just as a greenhouse keeps plants warm, greenhouse gases keep Earth warm.

COMPARE AND CONTRAST

What are some benefits of having the greenhouse effect? What are some drawbacks?

Earth's icy polar caps are white in this photo. The effects of global warming could melt the ice caps.

VOCABULARY

Deforestation is the clearing, or cutting down, of forests, often to make more room for farms, homes, and businesses.

Global warming is increased by deforestation. Trees absorb carbon dioxide, which is one of the greenhouse gases. Fewer trees mean that less carbon dioxide is being taken out of the atmosphere.

The effects of global warming could harm living things. The warmer temperatures could cause polar ice caps to melt. This would cause sea levels to rise. Plants, animals, and buildings along coastlines would be in danger. Many scientists believe that long-term droughts are another result of climate change.

Global warming is a worldwide concern. Governments are trying to limit the amount of greenhouse gases put into the air. Individual people can help by driving less. They can also save energy by turning off unneeded lights and other electrical devices. This will reduce the burning of fuel that releases greenhouse gases into the atmosphere.

One way people can reduce their impact on global warming is to use low-energy lightbulbs.

Pioneers of Weather and Climate

Weather and climate have a big impact on human life. Throughout history, there have been many people dedicated to studying these forces. Without their knowledge and inventions, daily life would be more difficult.

Aristotle wrote the first study on weather in the fourth century BCE. He was a philosopher in ancient Greece who wrote about many different subjects. His *Meteorologica* was widely studied by scholars for two thousand years.

Scholars, such as Aristotle, have studied weather and climate for thousands of years.

THINK ABOUT IT

Which development described here do you think changed people's lives the most? Why?

Daniel Gabriel Fahrenheit, a German scientist, invented the modern thermometer in 1709. Today, the United States and a few other countries measure temperature with the Fahrenheit scale.

People have always observed clouds. In 1803, meteorologist Luke Howard classified and named clouds by their appearance. His research helped meteorologists to make better weather predictions by connecting cloud formations to particular types of weather events.

Luke Howard's work on cloud formations has helped meteorologists predict weather for more than two hundred years.

29

GLOSSARY

atmosphere The layer of gases that surround Earth.

chemistry A science that deals with the substances that make up materials and the changes that take place when substances are combined.

condense To turn from a gas to a liquid.

decrease To make or become less.

drought A long period of dry weather.

equator An imaginary circle around Earth everywhere equally distant from the North Pole and the South Pole.

formation The manner in which a thing is formed, including its structure and shape.

fossil The remains of a plant or animal that lived long ago.

fuel A material used to produce heat or power by burning.

hail Small lumps of ice that fall from clouds sometimes during thunderstorms.

molecule The smallest particle of a substance having all the characteristics of the substance.

observation An act of gathering information by noting facts or events.

philosopher Someone who seeks wisdom by thinking about important questions.

physics A science that deals with the study of physical objects and the forces (pushes or pulls) that act on them.

predict To declare in advance on the basis of study, experience, or reasoning.

research The collecting of information about a subject.

satellite A human-made object or vehicle intended to orbit Earth, the Moon, or another heavenly body.

scholar A person who has done advanced study in a particular area.

For More Information

Books

Furgang, Kathy. *Everything Weather: Facts, Photos, and Fun that Will Blow You Away*. Washington, DC: National Geographic Children's Books, 2012.

Maloof, Torrey. *Climate* (Science Readers: Content and Literacy). Huntington Beach, CA: Teacher Created Materials, 2015.

Mattern, Joanne. *What Are Weather and Climate?* (Let's Find Out! Weather). New York, NY: Britannica Educational Publishing, 2015.

Sneideman, Joshua. *Climate Change: Discover How It Impacts Spaceship Earth* (Build It Yourself). White River Junction, VT: Nomad Press, 2015.

Steinberg, Lynnae. *What Is Weather Forecasting?* (Let's Find Out! Weather). New York, NY: Britannica Educational Publishing, 2015.

Websites

Because of the changing nature of internet links, Rosen Publishing has developed an online list of websites related to the subject of this book. This site is updated regularly. Please use this link to access the list:

http://www.rosenlinks.com/LFO/Climate

INDEX